THE BRECKER B...

...AND ALL THEIR JAZZ

Photography: Benno Friedman

ISBN 0-7935-6410-7

HAL•LEONARD®
CORPORATION
7777 W. BLUEMOUND RD. P.O. BOX 13819 MILWAUKEE, WI 53213

Visit Hal Leonard on the internet at http://www.halleonard.com

THE BRECKER BROS.

THE BAND

In 1975 the Brecker brothers were known as two of the top studio musicians in New York City: collectively they had contributed on the sessions of artists ranging from Janis Joplin, Stevie Wonder and Billy Cobham to James Taylor, Aretha Franklin and Laura Nyro. But when the opportunity came to record their first album with their own group, trumpeter Randy and saxophonist Michael went immediately into the studio. Randy remembers that "the idea of getting a band of our own together had been germinating since about 1973. It wasn't that we were tired of session playing because we always did live things here and there - it's just that the time seemed right after working with so many other people."

All the members of the band - which included (in various complements) saxophonist David Sanborn, keyboard player Don Grolnick, guitarists Bob Mann and Steve Khan, bassist Will Lee and drummer Christopher Parker - had been playing together either live or in the studio in one combination or another for almost five years. Their first two albums featured a wide variety of music, from hard-driving disco to more abstract jazz colorings and mellow vocal arrangements in the style of Stevie Wonder. Randy emphasizes that "we enjoy playing different kinds of music, depending on who we're playing with and for, because the band is really capable of playing in any direction. With the second album we have to be honest and say we're trying to appeal to as large an audience as possible. There's still a bit of the other - jazz - so people will remember who we are, but we've realized now that we have to be commercial as well."

JAZZ FANS

Growing up in Philadelphia, the Breckers both got into music at an early age. Randy (11/27/45) took up the trumpet in elementary school, but the orchestras there weren't very inspiring for him. Michael (3/29/49) picked up the clarinet at age 7, after listening to the clarinetists at the frequent jam sessions held by his piano-playing father.

After finishing high school both brothers went on to Indiana University, which offered a strong music program. Randy and Mike became great jazz fans: Randy's idols were Clifford Brown, Miles, Lee Morgan and Freddie Hubbard while Mike found inspiration in Cannonball, Coltrane, Sonny Rollins and Bird. After college Randy moved to New York, and he floated from band to band before winding up with the original Blood, Sweat and Tears. He only stayed for their first album, Child Is Father To The Man. From BS & T he joined Horace Silver, and at this time Michael made his way to the Big Apple.

PURE FORMS OF JAZZ

Together they formed Dreams, an avante-garde jazz-rock band that at one time or another included such prominent musicians as Billy Cobham and guitarist John Abercrombie. Dreams received great critical notices, but they couldn't make it commercially and, after two fine albums, the band broke up. Randy linked up with Larry Coryell's Eleventh House for its first album and, after that, both brothers performed with the Billy Cobham Band. All of this set the stage for the Brecker Brothers Band.

"When we formed the group we thought a lot about the kind of music we would play," says Randy. "The style of music we play now is really what we like doing, and after our background in more pure forms of jazz some people might find that hard to understand." Mike adds, "The music that we are playing now is an incorporation of our bebop influences."

They would like to be known as the top players in their genre of hybrid jazz-rock. "That's what we have in mind," smiles Randy. "Ideally we want to bring our audience into what we're doing with the plain funk - you know, semi-straight cooking R & B - then try and space it out a little with some abstract instrumental work."

In an era where many jazz musicians are tailoring their music for the mass audience, there have been the usual accusations that the Breckers have "sold out." But these critics are shortsighted - they forget the fact that the Breckers left very lucrative studio careers to forge ahead with the idea of their own band. Randy clarifies the point, saying "we don't really look at our music in those terms at all. You have to remember that you can't make records just for musicians alone. This is how we're going to be living the next ten years, so you just have to appeal to a wider audience. There's no other way to do it. But at the same time you have to keep in mind the music."

COLLECTIVE SPIRIT

Part of the Brecker Brothers' metamorphosis is their experimentation with electronic sounds to enhance their musical impact. The echoplex, the synthesizer and the wahwah pedal have all become part of the Brecker sound of the past few years. "The electronics are something we're going to continue to feel out and work on until we feel comfortable with it. We're experimenting with different kinds of electronic gadgets for the horns that are usually used on the guitar. I hope sometime people will get back into acoustic music, but it's exciting to see all that's happened with electricity."

The Breckers' music has enjoyed success because Randy and Michael have learned the difference between playing for live dates and working in the studio. "The combination of the two gives us the perspective we need to keep a lot of energy in the music. We have a certain repertoire, sure, but we keep it open so that the same people don't always play on the same tunes every night. There are a lot of things we can play live that we wouldn't record."

But, whether they're playing on the concert stage or in the studio, the Breckers constantly have to be aware of their music and the statement that it makes to the audience. "With this kind of band, if it becomes too harmonically oriented, it loses something. I guess to the average ear it sounds simple, but trying to make a commercial record is a lot harder than just aiming at a straight-ahead blowing type session."

THE SONGBOOK

The Brecker Brothers Songbook is filled with a spectrum of musical styles - at first glance the best place to start seems to be with the Breckers' hit single, "Sneakin' Up Behind You." The rhythm here is typical disco, and the bass and drums will be responsible for holding down the tight framework for the horn section to blow over. Both trumpet and sax have to pay close attention to the staccato riff they play - without this type of attack the song will lose its punch and go flat. The bass player must emphasize his descending line on the interlude following the bridge: this section offers a change of pace from the jackhammer drive of the beat and it has to be well-defined.

"Some Skunk Funk" features a very intricate opening - almost a trademark with Brecker compositions - as well as a very atypical chord progression during the song. This type of music could almost be termed "atonal disco" and it offers a challenge to the entire ensemble. The soloists may want to experiment with their improvising on this cut, since Randy's original playing here is so abstract.

The keyboard player on "Sponge" has to set the tempo immediately for the horn and rhythm section. The guitarist here will find a challenge in the Mahavishnu-like playing which embellishes the background. The bass, which solos in between verses, can't vary from its tempo or the entire band will find itself in confusion. One of the more uniques aspects of this song is the way the trumpet will solo during a verse, and the synthesizer will fall in behind it and answer the phrase. This type of dual improvising will improve the musical rapport that the ensemble will be working toward.

The opening of "A Creature Of Many Faces" is reminiscent of numerous free form jazz bands - once again it will be up to the keyboard player to segue out of this intro and into a rock solid rhythmic framework. Randy's playing on this composition recalls his stylistics with BS & T and Dreams - the trumpet player in the ensemble should work for these clear, open tones throughout the piece.

"Levitate" also features fine trumpet work, and with the floating waves of tremolo sound coming from the Fender Rhodes piano, the song shows the influence of Miles Davis circa *In A Silent Way*. The bass guitar takes on special importance in this song - it must define the tonics in this abstract chord progression and act as an anchor throughout the tune.

The rhythms on "Lovely Lady" are tricky: often the last beat of the measure is dropped to keep the song jumping, and all the musicians must be aware of the quick tempo shifts. This is a beautiful song, but its impact can be marred by a back-up section that lets the beat drag. Just because the composition is slow doesn't mean the bass and drums can forget the insistent pulse they have to create.

In updating their music to the current sounds of the times, the Brecker brothers have proven that "jazz" music (or at least jazz-oriented playing) can be accessible to a popular audience without compromising its quality.

They have put together the right elements of improvisation and well charted arrangements, of contemporary dance beats and experimental, often abstract instrumental work. The music is plugged into the zeitgeist, and it will change, evolve and grow as the years go by.

1977

Since the original publication of this book in 1977, the Breckers have enjoyed continued success, together and as solo artists. After a hiatus of nearly a decade, they reunited in 1992 for the GRP album *Return of the Brecker Brothers*, which earned three Grammy nominations. After a world tour, they returned to the studio in 1994 to record *Out of the Loop*, which won two Grammys – for Best Contemporary Jazz Performance, and Best Instrumental Composition for Michael's "African Skies." In 1996, each of the brothers released their first solo album in six years, with Michael's *Tales from the Hudson* released on Impulse Records (voted Jazz Album of the Year in December of '96 by Japan's Swing Journal, which also named Michael Jazz Man of the Year) and Randy's *Into the Sun* released on Pony Canyon in Japan and slated for release on Concord Jazz in the U.S. early in 1997.

1996

THE BRECKER BROS.
...AND ALL THEIR JAZZ

SNEAKIN' UP BEHIND YOU

Words and Music by
DON GROLNICK, WILL LEE, DAVE SANBORN,
RANDY BRECKER and MICHAEL BRECKER

SOME SKUNK FUNK

By RANDY BRECKER

TENOR - 2x, TRUMPET - 2x, After last
solo everyone TACET except Horns and
Drums who repeat bars 6 thru 9. BASS,
PIANO, & GUITAR enter on cue, then D.S.
to bar-4: play thru bar 45 and take CODA.

SPONGE

By RANDY BRECKER

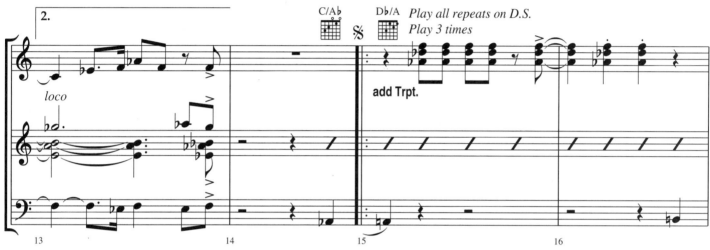

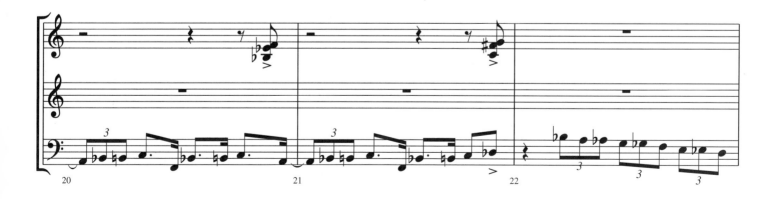

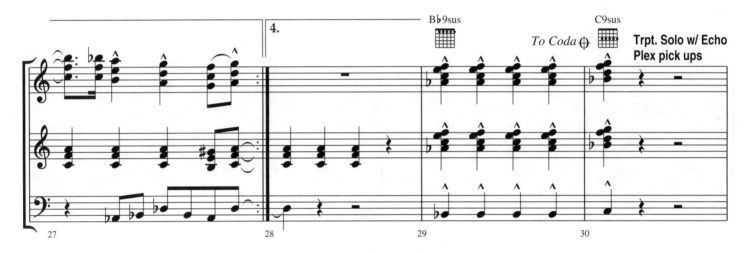

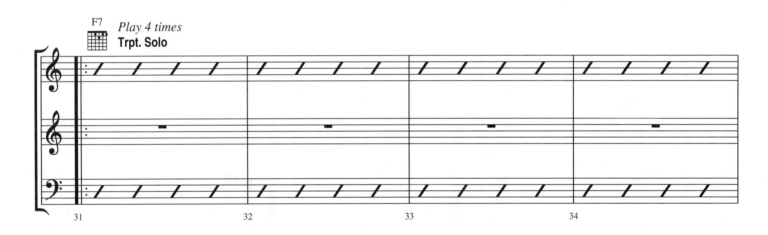

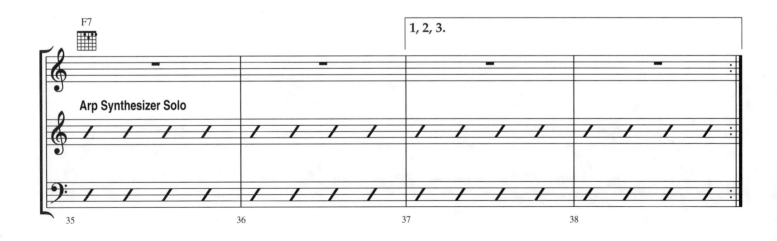

A CREATURE OF MANY FACES

By RANDY BRECKER

24

AT THE END OF SAX SOLO *play bars 61-68.*
AT THE END OF TRPT. SOLO *play bars 61-68.*
Then continue at G

LEVITATE

By RANDY BRECKER

LOVELY LADY

Words by ALLEE WILLIS, CHARLO CROSSLEY and DAVID LASLEY
Music by RANDY BRECKER

You made me love _ you Love-ly La - dy. _

Your love lights the day _ for me, _____

D.B.B.

By RANDY BRECKER

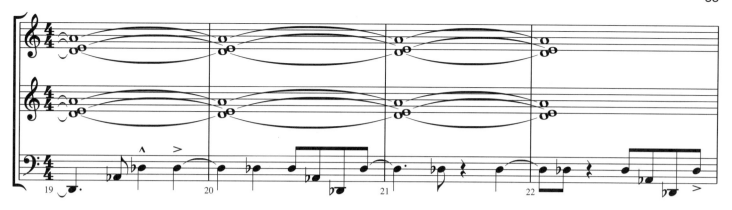

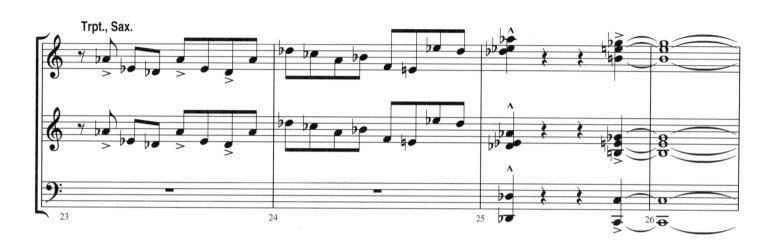

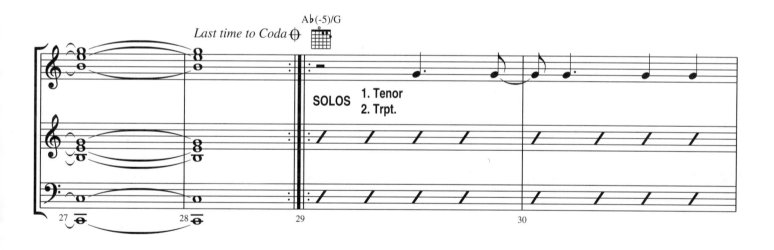

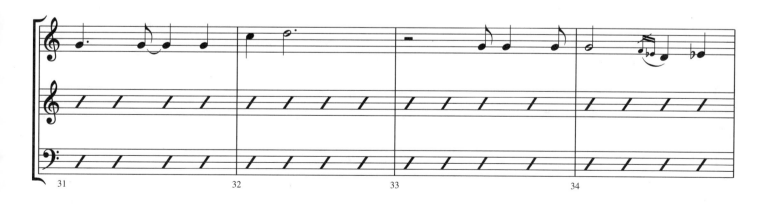

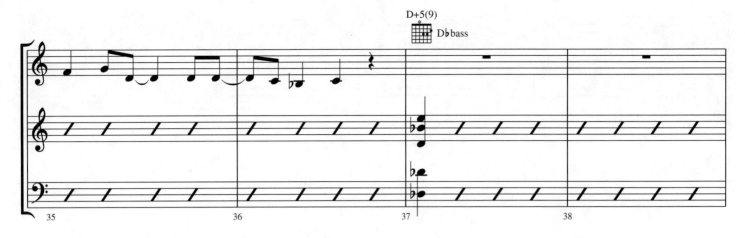

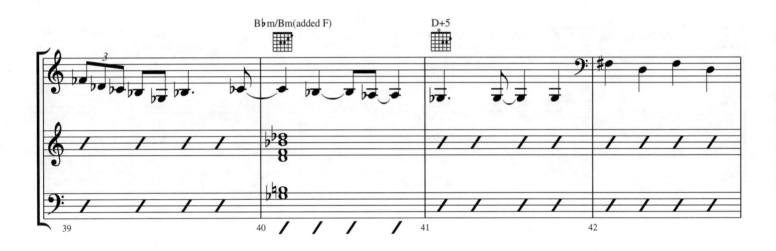

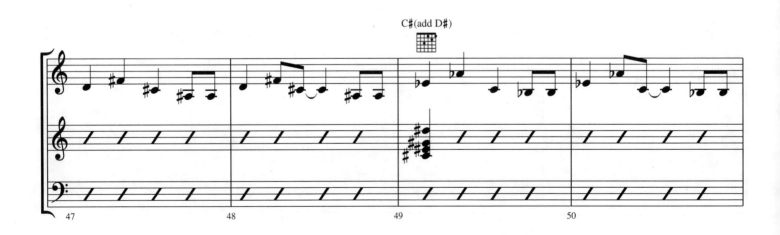

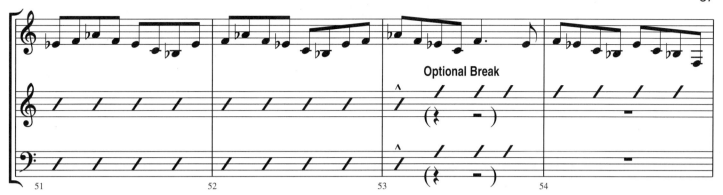

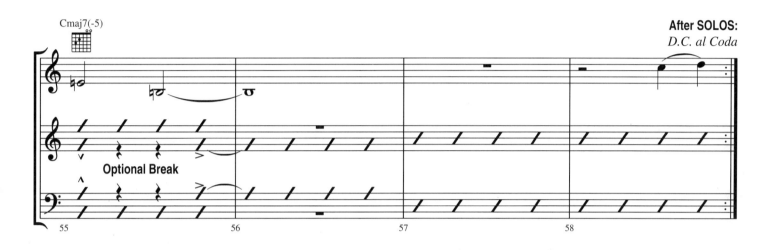

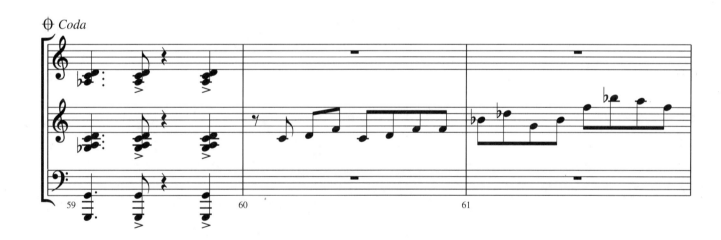

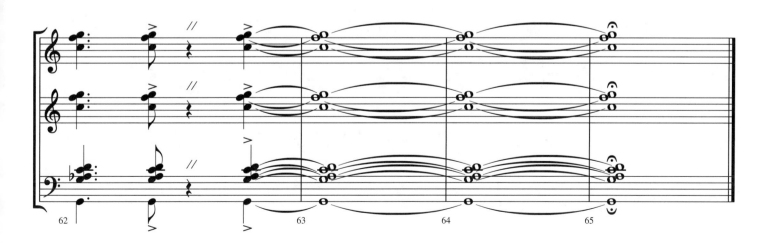

I LOVE WASTIN' TIME WITH YOU

Words by ALLEE WILLIS and CHARLO CROSSLEY
Music by MICHAEL BRECKER, ALLEE WILLIS
and CHARLO CROSSLEY

GREASE PIECE

By MICHEAL BRECKER, RANDY BRECKER
DAVE SANBORN and STEVE KHAN

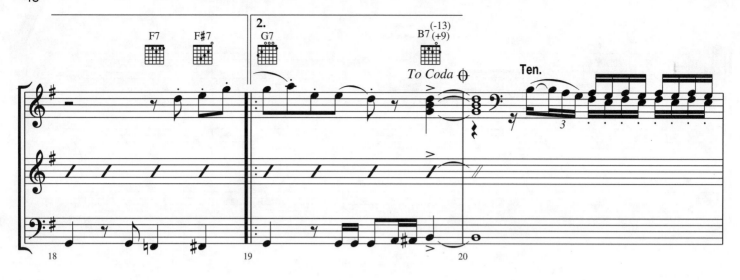

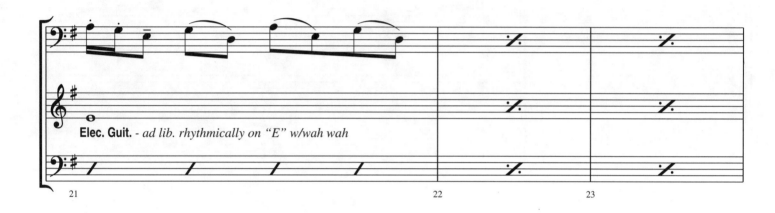

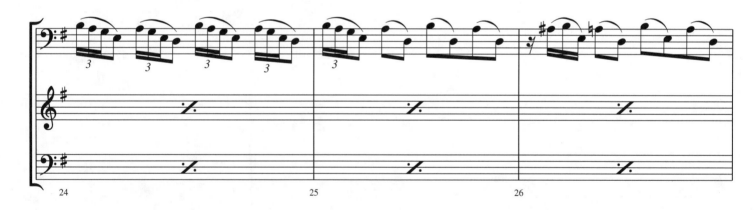

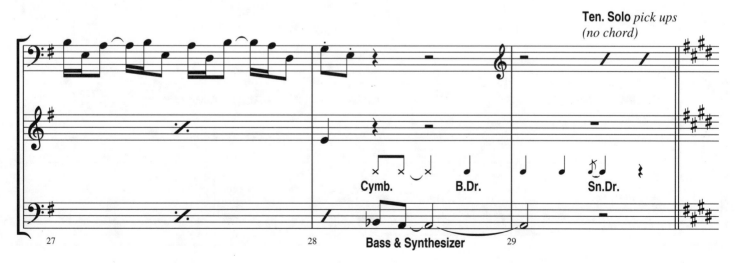

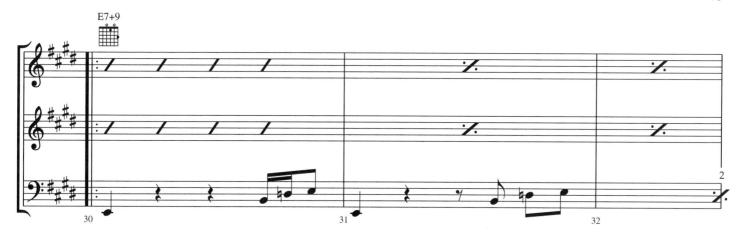

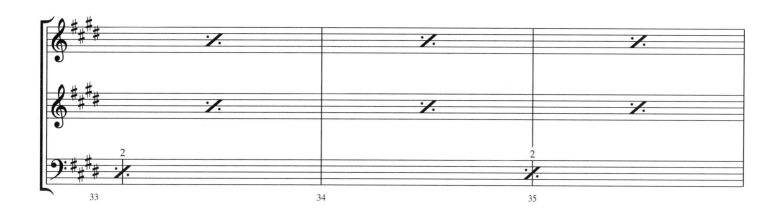

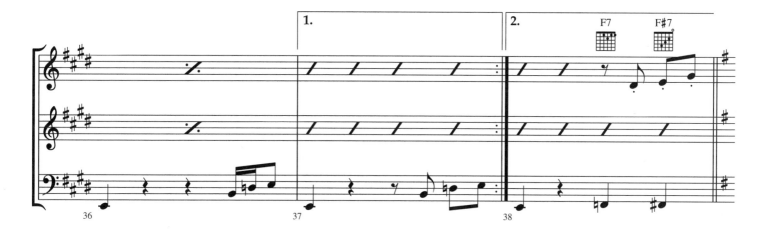

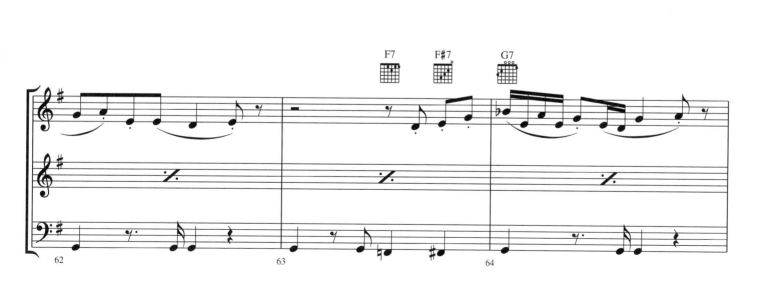

NIGHT FLIGHT

By MICHAEL BRECKER

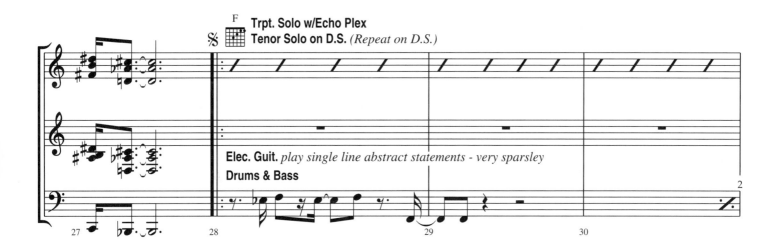

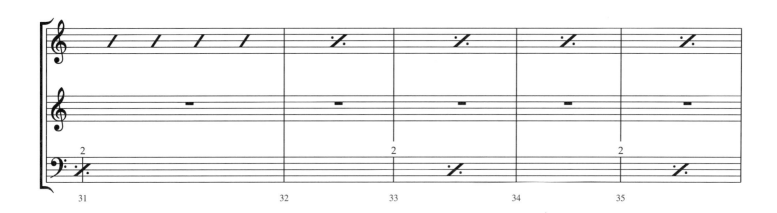

KEEP IT STEADY

Words and Music by
STEVE KHAN, RANDY BRECKER,
DAVID SANBORN and LUTHER VANDROSS

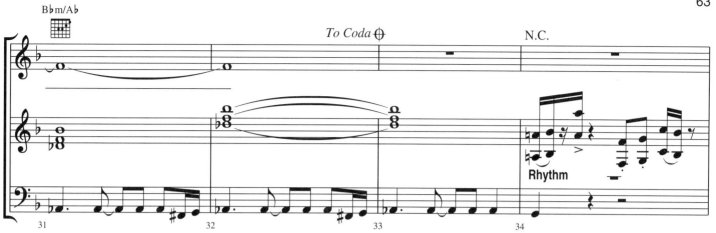

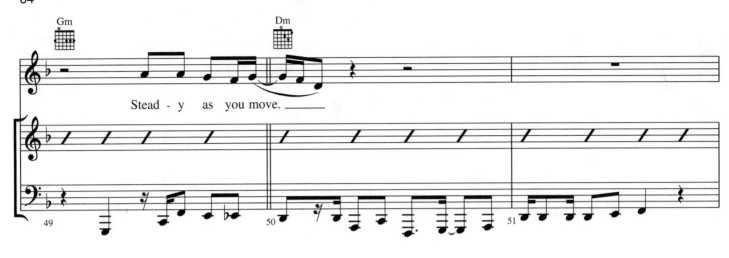

Stead - y as you move. _____

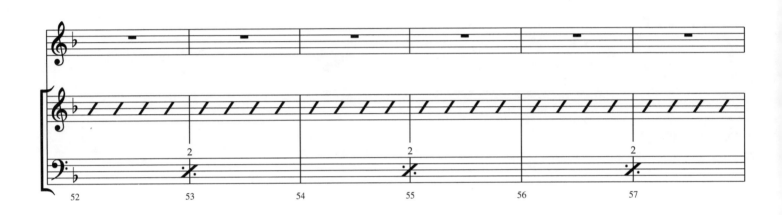

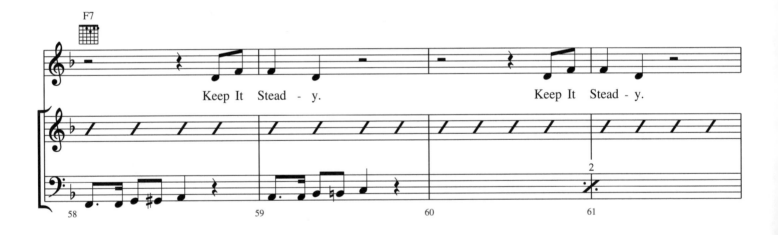

Keep It Stead - y. Keep It Stead - y.

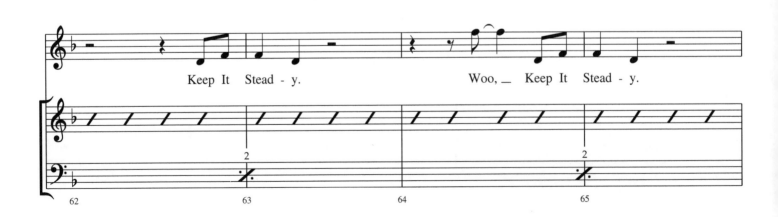

Keep It Stead - y. Woo, __ Keep It Stead - y.

OH MY STARS

By RANDY BRECKER

bris-tles in your hair and sun-shine in your stare what hap - pened?

Oh my stars _ what am I gon - na do?__ Oh my stars _

what am I gon-na do ____ with you ____

Oh I could leave _ you but I

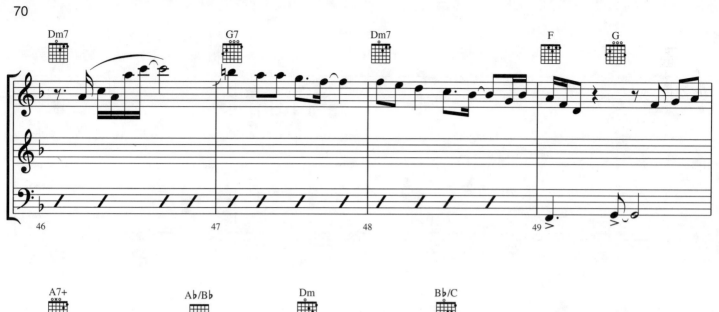

high fa-lu - tin' ways _ done got _ me think-in' I bet-ter start drink-in' and fast. _

Your high fa-lu - tin' gaze _ makes my heart start sink-in', my eyes. start blink-in' en -

ROCKS

By RANDY BRECKER

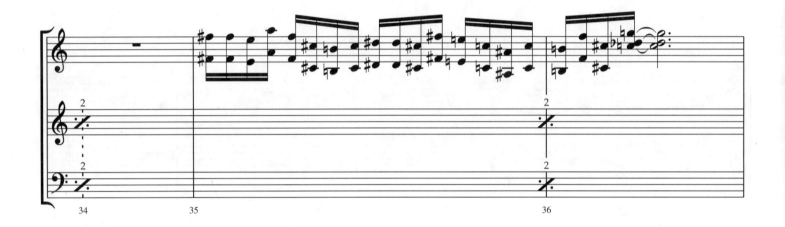

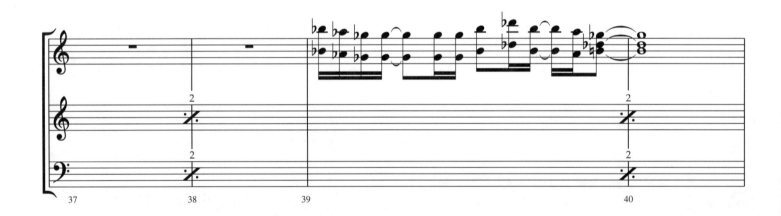

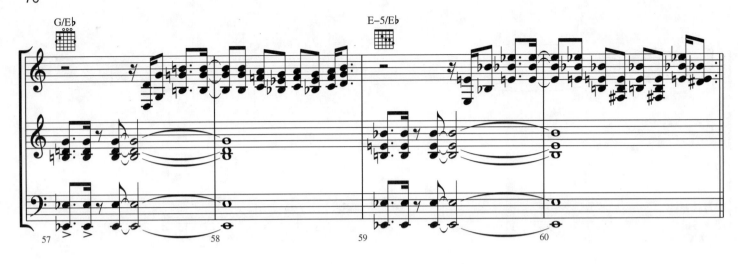

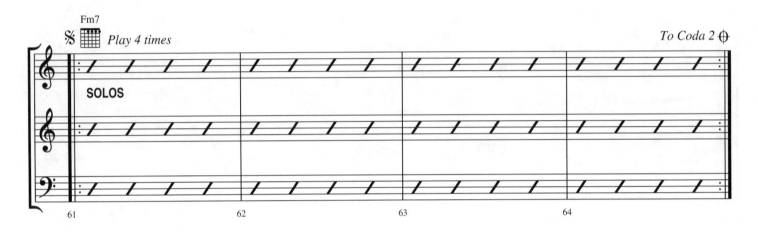

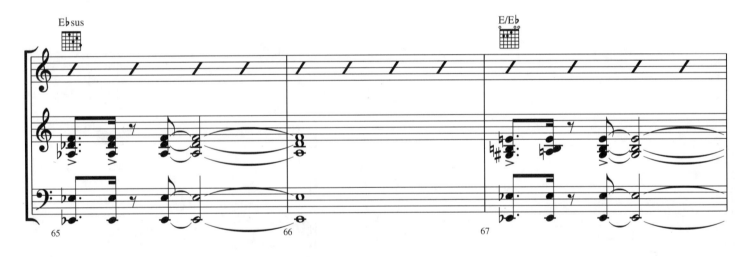

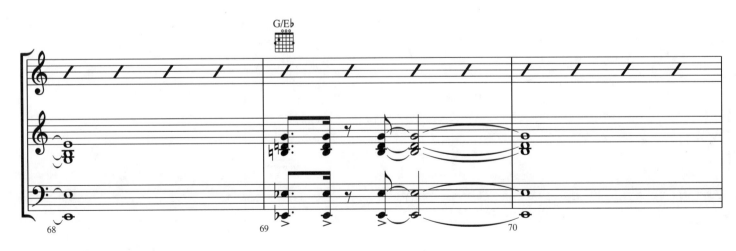

SLICK STUFF

By RANDY BRECKER

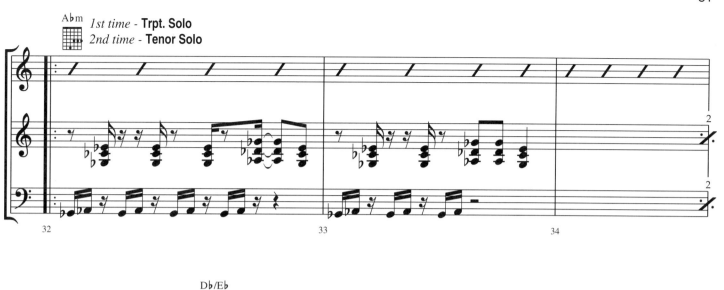

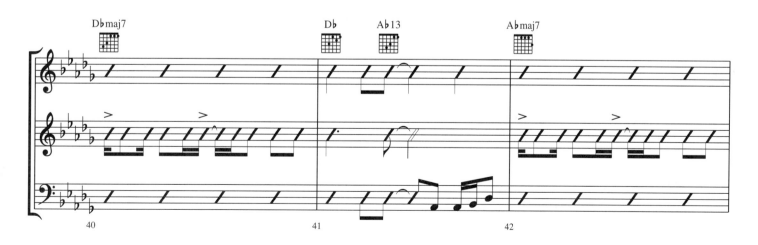

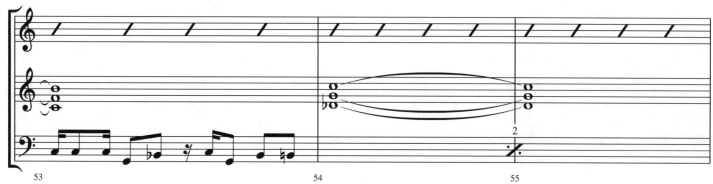

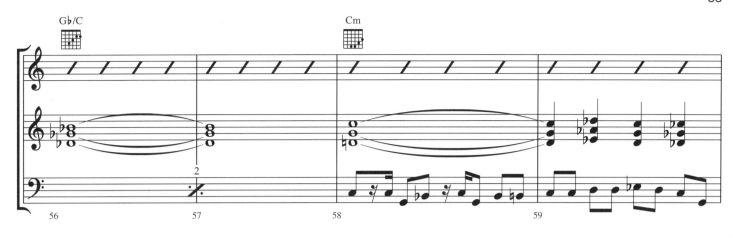

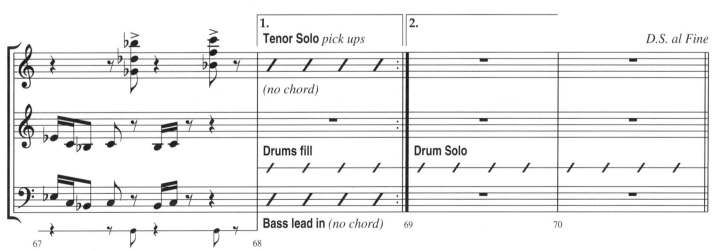

TWILIGHT

By RANDY BRECKER